the*fluent*
moment

To Eryl and Joyce Davies
and Des Carlill
absent friends

the *fluent* moment

Ruth Bidgood

seren

seren
is the book imprint of
Poetry Wales Press Ltd.
First Floor, 2 Wyndham Street
Bridgend, Mid Glamorgan
Wales, CF31 1EF

Cataloguing In Publication Data for this book
is available from the British Library

ISBN: 185411-170-1

*The publisher acknowledges the financial assistance of the
Arts Council of Wales*

Cover Art:
The Camarch Below Coedtrefan: Watercolour and pastel by Bernice Carlill.

Printed by: WBC Book Manufacturers, Bridgend.

Contents

The Fluent Moment

Against an inner wall of the small church
leans a symbol-stone, encapsulating
all things known, at rest. Sober-faced Sun,
rayed with crisp flames, is King of a static world.

But in the porch, ivy has climbed
right through the walls, insinuating
tough stems into crevices above the arch;
and flows high up in dark luxuriance,
forcing an over-shoulder glance, a thought
of all things built to fall, falling to rise.

The future has been and has been.
There is a movement here like Escley stream
that down from slopes of Cefn arrives
and in the same fluent moment leaves.

Up to the Twdin

There were vestiges of a path
alongside the river; most of our way
was pudging, slithering improvisation
over slimy stones, muddy roots.
The youngest happily fell into wet holes,
was hauled out, piggy-backed by his laughing father.
Sun on this day before Spring,
flicking through twigs, did not warm;
its hazy light left mystery intact,
as moonlight does. We crossed
on a tree-trunk bridge, some
scorning the one rail, some
inching sideways, eyes averted
from a few feet of drop.

High on the further bank, an old road through oaks
naked except for ivy and ruffling fern
ended in barbed wire by a gully.
We scrambled, slid, clawed,
gained open hilltop fields in brighter sun,
drew breath under blue sky, and saw in front
the ancient thing, the mound, the little twdin
with its rough peaky top, carved rocky ring
of ditch. One small boy rushed ahead,
round the ditch, up the last slope.
Right at his boots a rabbit started
and was gone. He flung up his arms,
amazed, ecstatic; shouted to us in joy.

Sun held us, held the child
calling from the high ground,
held the wide lonely land
stretching to the last circle of horizon.
I had a sense, keen, sudden, inexplicable,
of journeys, always beginning.

The Swift

There were prayers about famine. After,
lowering hymnbooks, children laughed,
their wildness released by a swift
that came dipping through the door,
sweeping to and fro, low over pews,
from font to altar and back.
For adults, dark rhythms of flight heightened,
not hid, pictures lodged in reluctant minds.

Up, up flew the swift. It would stay
for days unreachable, fall starved. Silhouetted,
clinging to the east window's topmost pane,
it drooped black angled wings symmetrically
over glories of suffering and triumph,
seeming to offer mutely, in doomed grace,
blackest of shadows for images of shelter.

Siân Fach

'Little Jane', they called her, 'Siân fach'.
'A proud little woman',
said her English daughter-in-law,
who never felt well in Conwy —
something to do, she thought, with the hills,
too near, too big, stealing the best of the air.
Something to do with Siân fach, too,
the little spendthrift widow,
petted and subsidised
by her four sons, and slaved for
by her one resentful daughter.

Always a huddle of Welsh
chuntering in corners, family talk
never fully translated, sounding
crisis-laden. Little Jane was polite
to the foreign bride, speaking to her
occasionally, in careful English —
an aristo attempting patois
for the benefit of a well-disposed
but regrettable connection,
of a lesser breed.

I have a photograph of Siân,
still dark-haired, stiffly trim in black.
Small, old and queenly, chin uptilted,
she sits throned on a wooden chair
at the top of stone steps outside
her ancient house. Standing at her side,
looking apologetic, is a courtier
halfway back into favour, the son
who brought home a stranger.

          His bride, of course,
is not in the picture. If there was
any contest, it is she, I suppose,
who won, remaining a visitor only,

and not a frequent one; seeing to it
that her family's roots were plunged
into warm coaly earth of the South,
with its more manageable hills
and uncensorious jumble of language.

Siân, you died before I was old enough
to be taken North. What would you make
of a granddaughter tripped
by the rocks of your language,
a great-grandson not of the North
yet bonded to its mountains?
Apart from that photograph,
all I ever had of you
was an ormolu clock that got lost or sold,
and whatever sawdusty treasures
I dipped from the mysterious
lucky tub of your genes.

Let us not judge each other.
If I put away your photograph,
it's not to disown proud little Siân,
only to keep from fading,
another year or two,
that record, that faint sepia memory.

Away from Home

The Irish doctor and his wife
lived their expatriate rôle
to the last quirk and syllable.
Seven years old, I could see
but not define their strangeness.

Not knowing brandy, I had no name
for that dominant note in the close
heavy-perfumed room.

            I liked the parrot,
its slowly-tilting head, its aged critical eye,
half-human raucous talk.

            I liked the doctor,
who said little, chewed on his pipe, stared out
(sadly, I thought) over back-to-back rows
to the hills.

            Most, I liked his wife, her desperate
un-Welsh, un-English chatter, the one curler
often forgotten among tight rolls
of shiny black hair, her startling beads,
the way she would tip a bottle
over her teacup, turn on
a scrapy gramophone, and plumply jig,
reaching out to her husband, who made
only a small disclaiming gesture.

I think that even then I sensed
the doctor and his wife were away from home
for ever (since home, if they returned,
would not be what they wanted), and that they
knew this, and could not be healed.
I sipped the too-sugary tea, and tried to dance.

Moving

Moving in old age, she lived for a while
in debatable land, her disorientation
not so much frightening as baffling.
The new house was what she wanted —
she was sure of that. She would laugh
at her own mistakes — opening the wrong door,
momentarily forgetting where to find
cupboards. The other house still seemed hers,
shadowing the new one. Heavy
with years of her past, it outweighed
her frail thin life in this new dwelling,
fresh growth that might not reach maturity.

Before long, she was certain she had crossed
a border. She was learning the small
idiosyncrasies of her house, its rattles and taps,
misfits and slants: where sun first warmed,
last lingered. Even dislikeable corners
were becoming everyday and her own.
With no conscious resolve, she made such knowledge
a marking of territory, a coming home.

Encounter

He had taken the wrong road, he said,
baffling, with its twists, retreats
upon itself, dips and climbs, all the time
carrying him further into hills,
ending in the yard of a farm, remote
from any life he'd thought still possible.
Clean window-panes of a low white house
danced with the last of sun.
The outmoded tractor was a treasure
in its well-patched shed.
Hens high-stepped, unworried,
tilting neat heads. From his dung-heap
their red master called.

An old man and his wife came out to talk.
One story of theirs he remembered. Up in the rafters
the old farmer had found an ancient saddle,
a lady's saddle, fringed and tooled.
As he bore it into sharp, sunny air,
it lost shape, was other, was nothing,
powdering into dust, blowing away.
That had seemed a right conjunction
of time, place, event. Was there something, too,
even less for the seizing, a cloud of dust,
whirling up, high, higher, gone away?

Up-Country

'Oh, you're up-country folk, then',
said he, when we responded
to his ritual curiosity.
(His own sloping fields were hardly,
some would think, lowland; mountains
bigger than our moorland hills
distantly reared against blue sky).

I liked this pigeon-holing, enjoyed
a little swagger of the spirit.
'Up-country'; he said it with respect.
Leaning on the gate of his great yard
with its long whitewashed house,
ancient stone barns, he narrowed his eyes,
savouring a notion of eccentricity,
endurance; of something out-on-the-edge;
of folk (how flattered, he little knew!)
living the stuff of tall tales.

Bluetit Feeding

Early at the window in starved winter
a little knot of energies, a beaky hunger
fluffed and sleeked, taps, prises
unsucculent scraps of cracked putty,
swallows with a ripple of tiny throat.

Behind it climbs a bleak pale hill
stained with rust of December bracken.
White morning moon is barely seen
on hardly darker sky that seems
opaque, a barrier against pressure
of immensities. Imperceptibly
the chill day flows out to black deeps.

The bluetit pauses in its arid feeding,
flirts a crisp wing. Half-handful of warmth,
it stays for a moment still,
compellingly centre-stage, diminishing
to a backdrop the hill, dull morning sky,
pale echo of moon, black vertiginous
trenches of space-ocean, myriads
of molten and frozen, dying and rising worlds.

Dancers

This is the little tea-house
of the children, the admiral's daughters.
Anyone can walk now in their garden
high above the bay. Anyone can take,
if they find it, the narrow path
to the gabled octagon, climb stone steps,
try the locked door. Each wall is windowed;
anyone can look in, look across to the sea.

The three daughters of the admiral
chattered, sipped the tea servants carried
over the lawn. One day they danced
round and round their sunny picnic-room,
danced frantically as through they would never stop.
Eight windows let sky, leaves, sea
whirl with them, unforgettably.

Round and round they dance, the children.
There they go, dancing, whirling, the admiral's daughters —
one married and away, one dead and gone, one
lost, lost — round and round their picnic-room
in the empty tea-house.

Six Houses

1. Harp at Glanbrân

For years after the fire
the ruin reared up on meadow-land,
tall fragments of façade,
some broken rooms,
all that was left of the empty palace
where Gwynne after lordly Gwynne
had reigned for generations.

The last one had deer in the park,
flower-beds on the roof,
four-in-hand coach kept furbished
for rattling, half-royal journeying
up to the turnpike and away.

A few tiptoe intruders
in teetering roofless rooms
thought they heard a harp in the wind —
Sackville's tame harpist from the North
trying out his host's new song.
Now and then the peacocks
would scream suddenly, jolt his hand,
and send a discord jangling down the years.

'A perfect and a splendid ruin',
said a reporter, 'though slightly out of repair'.
Fire wrote an unkinder sentence. Demolition
has left an image reared against the clouds,
a shriek and jangle in corridors of air.

(Sackville Gwynne of Glanbrân loved the harp, entertained
harpists, and himself wrote music for the instrument.)

2. Kilvert Visits Penoyre

'Only twenty-five bedrooms', said the diarist,
disappointed with their small size
and the darkness of the billiard room.
He didn't see it at its best (the old Colonel
was five years dead, fading impoverished
at the Bear in Brecon; and the whole place
was peeling). Why couldn't he talk about
the views? — east to the Black Mountains,
westward to Usk and more hills, south
to wooded Benni and the Beacons? All that
mattered more, didn't it, than deal pillars
(that should have been marble) and the rest
of the 'sham hollow work' (fun for the Colonel,
and crumbling anyway by 1870)?

Down fields and a shady ride he found the lake,
one end reed-choked, the other channelled
towards the river, and 'rippling heavy and muddy'
like local stories. It was the fishing-lodge
that took his fancy; he was disapproving
and fascinated. 'Wild strange work'! He told
only of carriages waiting all night,
bursts of fireworks over the boats on the lake,
dancing in the ballroom until morning.
The rest stayed in his mind. Still,
what he left out could hardly have surprised,
however mixed his feelings, a man
who knew the 'angel satyr' on the hill.

(Kilvert's diary entry for 20 June 1871 is 'An angel satyr walks
these hills'.)

3. Catherine at Stouthall

It must be the yellowest house in Wales!
What would John Lucas, who made it grow
in Palladian dignity from the old
farmhouse of his kin, think of this
mustard ostentation? No sure answer; he had
his quirks and whims. Yet this insistent colour
would not suit Catherine, daughter of shadow,
his dark-haired wife with melancholy eyes.

Could her Gower neighbours have met the bride
without a whisper in the mind, 'Glanareth'?
without a sickened scenting of her father's
spilt blood in that old house in hills to the north?
(And what had the delectable mother known? —
gone with her lover, and dragging two daughters
on her dubious journeying?) Perhaps
this dark girl kept a distance, let the quiet
of her coastland home, the structure of affection
and obligation, measured progress through
a given life, work on her mind. Or perhaps
that other mansion and its mayhem seemed
a half-heard story, not her own at all,
and neighbours' speculations were hardly noticed,
powerless to break the calm.

             Her pictured face
is unreadable. It is hard to hold
the thought of her together with today's
exuberance of colour. She is more akin
to black water, deep grass, the dark of trees
swaying in winds not always off the sea,
but reaching out from far-off northern hills.

(Stouthall is no longer a yellow house; it was repainted in 1993.
The Glanareth murder in 1770 was a cause célèbre. John Powell
was killed by a group of men which included his wife's lover.)

4. Sweetness (Trefeca Fawr)

Overhead, plaster is joyous
with ferment of fruit, opulence of harvest.
This was his farm, the Preacher.
Dizzy with the Word, he could still
contain the crowd's excess.
What need of earth's honey?
A man threw away his harp,
a girl gave up dancing. Sweetness,
we have had great sweetness, they gloried.

But on his farmhouse ceilings
is the land's praise and challenge.
No end here to leaves' dance;
they whirl in still white while the house lasts.
Silence holds endless harvest music.
Up there in swag, row, cluster, flaunt
in profusion sweet, sweet apples
for the longing mouth.

(The Calvinistic Methodist evangelist, Howell Harries of Coleg
Trefeca, rented Trefeca Fawr as a farm from his brother Thomas.)

5. Erddig

Back in the bus, the talk was not so much
of the long plain house, its motley treasures,
renascent grounds; but of the servants' portraits,
those live and diverse faces,
and the Yorkes' affectionate doggerel,
breaking the green baize barrier.
Something else, too, would stay with me —
an echo of threat, a flavour of dereliction.
Rescued, this is a Lazarus of a house,
that went into dark, and remembers it.
Dark shuddered in workings
below the foundations, rained down
on carpet and canopy, seeped into
the flickering room where Simon Yorke
dined in gumboots. Nearby in the saloon
grubby ewes came in from the jungle garden
to pudge the floor, startle at splashes
and mirror-gleams. Shored up now,
spruced and lit, the house still holds
a hint of precariousness, as though it said
'Whither all tends, I already know;
whence I returned, there I shall go'.

(The Yorkes of Erddig collected paintings and photographs of
their servants from the 18th century on, and wrote verses about
some of them. The mansion was rescued from subsidence due to
mine-workings.)

6. Beaupré Castle

How is it possible to forget so much?
We came chattering out of the lanes
St Hilary way. Beaupré, Bewper —
not a castle then, not a ruin. In the old
stone kitchen warmed by a summer fire
I sat and laughed with the rest, all of us young;
I was the stranger, welcomed and quizzed.
Three daughters of the farm poured tea.

The two great porches I know now
from books, but don't remember.
Then, there was arching dark
after the white lane, an ancientness
growing from the rough utilitarian garden,
grandeur comfortably mixed
with everyday, all just a stage-set
for a dance of happiness over shadows.

I should have liked to think of Richard Bassett
building his storeyed porch, and wonder
how much truth Iolo put into his legends.
I should have read the words in stone,
'Say couldst thou ever find
or ever hear or see
worldly wretch or coward prove
a faithful friend to be?'
                                    But that
was for another time, not this
tunnel-visioned, unregretted afternoon,
when the parched lanes offered up
puffs of white dust, and grey dank walls
softened and held our taut excited laughter.

(The poet and antiquary Iolo Morgannwg's stories about Beaupré
and its families are characteristically unreliable.)

Starlings

The top of the Douglas fir is dead —
a third at least of its huge height.
The lawn darkens; behind the trees
the sky is white still, but losing
luminosity. Suddenly,
a great dispersal of starlings
wheels chittering and skirling
high over the garden, condenses,
funnels down to the great fir,
noisily settles on the dead branches
in a controlled flurry of feathery
balletic changes and resolutions.

Coming home near dusk, in the distance
I see the dead tree burgeon with score on score
of black vibrating fir-cones, and hear
a rushing sound like the sap of the world
irresistibly rising.

Snake

'Would you like to hold my favourite snake?'
My fear (remembering Lawrence's 'pettiness')
was of committing a solecism. The snake
seemed untroubled. She was a slender length
of softly mottled brown, firm, dry and warm —
a boa-constrictor. She had been coiled
on her heating-pad, digesting rat-pups,
and might have been tetchy, but today
was patient of human touch,
twining round my hands,
her dainty head turning, searching.
I understood as never before
the cliché of eyes like beads,
for yes, hers were two tiny dark beads,
lidless lenses sloughed and renewed
with her skin. Soon her front half
sailed gracefully over air
to reach the boy she knew, making
the outline of an ancient ship
with seeking prow; then the rest of her
slipped through my fingers. She left
a momentary tingle on the skin,
a small stretching, flexing of known things
towards the incalculable and alien.

Through Binoculars

I turn the knurled ring; the top field
blurs, sharpens. Identified,
a buzzard stares from its post
as if into my eyes.
That is another country,
hill rising more steeply,
woods massing darkly
in unfamiliar proportion.

Always the lens, plastic or glass,
the tough jelly of the eye,
the mind's distortion.
Through my binoculars,
my imperfect eyes,
my struggling mind,
I stare; with illusory
complicity, the buzzard's eyes
meet mine, as if we shared,
one moment, a view of the world.
Then with slow power its wings
lift; it soars beyond my lenses' reach.

Deer in Wyre Forest

for Amy

We went into the forest, looking for deer.
Even when we started, light was failing;
but this was her home patch — she held my hand
politely, not for reassurance.
She knew the landmarks: the huge cleared swathe
where a pipe-line struck out cross-country,
the treetop hide, the side-path into dark
(a good place for toadstools).
                    When we reached
the observation post, it was closed.
We peered through glass at posters,
half-visible, and across the glade
to the further tree-fringe, hoping
for the lithe wariness of homing deer.

As we turned to go, rain-clouds
thickening dusk, a flick of movement
caught us. We looked back. Over the clearing,
dim at the forest edge, was a shape, shadow,
a thing poised, a presence that distantly
skittered and snuffed.
A deer, we said, and set out content
for the dark return between dense trees
to the lights of her father's car.

I can't find that walk in my diary.
For years she may not find it in memory —
perhaps not till she is old
will something startle one day from hiding
the shapes of that evening. There, suddenly,
will be the doe in the dusky glade,
secret at the forest verge, homing.

Hare at Pennant

The ancient life-symbol of the Hare became debased over the centuries. One of its later manifestations, the Trickster, is in this poem identified with the hare saved by Saint Melangell from the hounds of Prince Brochwel in an ancient Latin Ms copied in the 17th century.

I Hare have been the clever one,
up to my tricks, always a winner,
fooling man and beast — but not now,
not you, pretty lady, holy one.
You untwist my deviousness.
I huddle at your feet
in your garments' folds,
and am simple hare, fool hare, hunted hare.
I have doubled and doubled,
am spent, blown, not a trick left
to baffle pursuers.
A leap of despair
has brought me to you.

Cudd fi, Melangell,
Monacella, hide me!

*

'Seize him!' I cried to my hounds
(the best, I had thought, in all
my princedom of Powys).
But each time I chivvied them on,
the fools came squealing and squelking back.
So I rode into tanglewood,
my huntsmen after me,
the wretched scruff-hounds skulking off;
and she was there in the glade,
still as an image, still
as her carved Christ on his cross.
I pictured her alone with me;
but this was no girl from the huts
to be gripped and thrown aside
for a paltry coin, no absent warrior's
hungry wife. Cool as moonlight

this maiden waited on wet grass,
looking up at me with no fear, no blame,
and by her small bare feet,
panting and peeping, crouched the hare.

I saw how it would be; she'd get her land
from me, the prayer-girl, to make
a sanctuary here — and Powys
would go short of hare-meat
and the dark strong broth! I
would make my peace with the cringing dogs,
hunt forests to the north for other prey,
yet leave a thought behind me here
for her to shelter.

Cudd fi, Melangell,
Monacella, hide me!

*

Once I was Great Hare
and the Moon's companion,
and Easter's acolyte bearing the light.
Victim, I ran charred through heath-fire,
lay bloodied in last corn.
I was warped to hold the soul of a witch:
dwindled to trickster and buffoon.
Men dodge my real, unchancy name,
calling me cat-shanks, cabbager,
dew-fellow, cat-of-the-furze,
maze-maker, leaper-to-hill.
False, broken is my boast of winning;
I crouch in dread of the fangs.
All I have been, am, she shelters.
'Not I', she says, 'it is my Lord'. But she
is what I know, soft-robed saint,
gentle one, who heard my piping cry,

Cudd fi, cudd fi, Melangell,
Monacella, hide me!

Memorial

The cloisters were not silent.
Prayers for peace, from depths of the cathedral,
came faintly along the arcades.
A door had a notice pinned, 'Do not disturb
the practice'. Prentice choirboys
wobblingly essayed high notes. Slightly off-key,
a descant filtered through dull wood.
At the stone walkway's end shone green
a sunny lawn; from a swing
a child squealed and chortled.

I was looking for a name,
a house, date, identity; and found,
high on the wall, the right memorial.
Here he was — baby, husband, father:
who helped some, cheated others,
built with pride, lost much, died poor.

Craning to read the lettered stone,
I heard voices of the present — child's laugh,
flawed singing, susurration of prayer; and felt
the reality of the life recorded here
too high for easy reading.
                        Walking away,
I listened to jumbled speech
in the deep of my mind, hearing over and over
a word that sounded like 'sleep'.

Feast

Victorian church, Victorian Week — the theme
is 'Legends'. Here sits Cewydd,
saint of weather, seeming to accept
benignly the likelihood of rain.
Nearby, a girl who has dressed the well
peeps coyly into its cold secretness,
coaxing the depths to predict her man.

Visitors file by, caught by printed cards
with chilly Radnorshire stories: of three brothers
each clasped in the others' rigid embrace
under the mountain snow, of hauntings
on frozen Llyn Gwyn, of a girl
who fell face down on Llyn Heilyn's ice
and through it saw dead eyes stare up at her.

The side-aisle café is full. Two Italian girls,
two men and a push-chair squash into a corner,
laughing; save sliding tea-cups, pass
across the table a dark-eyed baby,
beautiful and merry. All that warmth,
vividness, the cuddly frilly child,
bursting laughter, join with the cold
ancientness of local story to heighten
the faceted shining of a little feast.

Llwybrau Gynt

(Former Paths)

Small road dwindles to track, to path,
to ripple in bracken. Jettison the map;
it has lost fifty years. Long ago,
passenger on another journey,
intent on another map, I coaxed you
to go bumping over fields and venture
into the shadow of a track.
We careered crazily down, dark trees
encroaching on our stony way.
At a giddy bend, I just caught sight,
with disproportionate elation,
of a red eye gleaming from underbrush,
shining studs of a blackened, battered marker,
forgotten as long as the tiny road
of whose asperities it had warned.

Now again a faint line in bracken
seems part of an incomplete pattern.
Something challenges, daring me to imagine
unimaginable destinations
for unreturning ways.

Mountain Road

Sarn Helen traversed these flats and foothills,
but we are heading for an older road.
Almost as soon as there were men to walk it
the road was there across the plateau, falling giddily
into valleys, clutching its way back up:
narrow, uncompromising.

Rain blurs the dingy green of winter fields,
the distant patch of grey that is the town. Beyond,
true hills begin, black today, magnified.
Surely it is we who invent portentousness
in earth's unmeaning bulk?

Yet late in this clammy day, as we turn up
into rainy wilderness, that thought falters.
There comes a blurring of boundaries.
All fought over, suffered, aspired to, loved —
here, there: then, now — seems one with what we write,
this moment, on the barren hills' dark page,
out of the depths of our uncharted minds;
and what we feel now is the ancient awe.

Gigant Striding

Leland, heading south for Rhaeadr
through wilderness, crossed over Claerddu,
no great streame but cumming thoroug cragges.

Between two little hills
a gigant striding was wont to wasch his hondes,
till Arthur killed him, for no reason known.

Perhaps it was just for his gigantic
striding, that diminished the moor;
his great hands commandeering the stream —

for being huge, anarchic; sharing
ancientness and threat
of the desolate land.

Claerddu, clear black. Unchanging
miles of soggy moor. Small plash
of the stream in a basin of stone.

The dwellers say also that the gigant
was buried therby, and shew the place.
A vast shadow hovers and is gone.

Holiday Path

1. Up the Hill

Stumbling up the rocky gradients
of a disused road, slippery and riverlike
that rain-logged winter, we came
to the holiday path that darkly climbed
into forest. Victorian planners cut
these narrow zigzags on the open hill
to offer guests a prospect of the spa.

Those great skirts Kipling heard
swishing along his 'old lost road'
would hush and rustle here, if they came again,
over a stair-carpet of tawny needles
impacted in many seasons, and broken
on dizzy corners by root or rock.

Trees by the thousand hide the prospect now,
except from a high clearing at the edge
of forest. We saw below the small grey town
fuzzy in rain, and far-away hills
too blurred by mist to name with certainty.

I remember a narrow, intense
downward glimpse, between firs, of an older tree,
huge, leafless, that lit a turn of the track
with the cold silky gleam of pale
enveloping moss. It had an otherness,
like the brush of long skirts on today's path,
or a Victorian girl on the zigzag climb
up the bare hill, suddenly pausing,
nervous hand to throat, feeling shut in by trees.

2. Under the Chalets

The peat goes deep. Chalets
are up on blocks; below,
sunk foundations, and a J.C.B.
that went down years ago,
ineluctably settling,
glugging into black depths.

Families holiday here,
pattering and clunking over floors
clamped to bars of concrete.
Now and then the curious hear stories.
It would be wild to say they sleep
less easily (after all that walking,
or soft drunk air of fishing afternoons).

Only, once in a while, there comes
a sense of rigid forms
uneasily lodged below in acid earth,
and, further, much further down, whatever
for centuries sank through fathoms of the unknown.

Cracks

In Penylan Road, Dinas Road, Pendref,
pavements are cracking. People there
grumble, but are not much perturbed
at this little encroachment of chaos.
Washing cars, weeding paths, they cherish,
as long as they may, all
controllable things, and go on
making small memories.

Pavements are cracking. The lines form a pattern
like rivers or roads on maps. Here and there
through the cracks creep small plants,
embellishments such as old cartographers
added in corners and margins —
pygmy beasts, fruits, cherubs, flowers,
to complement their hazardous projections
with forms of tenacious life.

Land

1. The Song

The farm grew its own small wood
of tall conifers. Gales thinned them;
some teetered, roots ripping upward,
but could only lurch on to thin,
close-packed neighbours, making with them
precarious arches.

From fields above to fields below,
down through the wood's dimness, plunge
long mounded lines, lost enclosures' boundaries.
Digging, dragging, heaving, firming:
sun-sweat, snow-shiver: man and hill,
and the years turning, turning
on to dark trees, and hidden mounds
delimiting sour garths.

        But at the wood's lower edge
expansive sweet-chestnuts drop their splayed fruit;
above, where sidelan fields border on hill,
is a beech-glade, gold now, hazed
with a haunting of bluebells in late spring,
intenser here than anywhere — a marginal,
useless acreage, where now
once-disregarded beauty carries
the song of the place.

2. Ploughing Team

First acre for the ploughman,
if he can make a plough
from first nail to last.

Second acre for the keeper
of the irons, sharpener
of ploughshare and coulter.

Two acres for the owners
of the outermost oxen,
lest the yoke be broken.

An acre each for the owners
of the inner oxen, graded
in pride of years and strength.

The singing acre for the caller,
who brings the yoke,
who yokes the oxen with due care,
who calls them, who all the hours
of their labour chants to them
lest their hearts break.

The black acre for the man
whose ox drops in the yoke,
its heart breaking,
its breath fading over the furrows,
death calling it away.

3. Cenfaes

This is a still place.
The breeze huffs and puffs tinily,
an irrelevance. Below the hill
the stream is hidden, its chatter muted.

It was hard to find the way here.
Since I came last, a generation
has been born and grown. New spurs of forest
confuse direction. In old fields
new leys have come and gone.
Slimy wood of an old gate lies in a ditch;
new wire, steel-thorned, stretches taut
from post to fresh-cut post.

The house is no more decayed
than thirty years ago.
It has borrowed an adventitious life
from vegetation — fir-tree pressing up
to the gable-end, tangle of grass and leaf
in open rooms. The land is grazed,
erratically; even the forest,
darkly, sourly flourishing, was planned
and brought to birth. Across the valley
a gleam of white is a rebuilt house,
grey sheen a new barn.

Those who lived up here
must have known stillness like this,
a pause in the land's long story, when the mind
accepts loss and looking-forward,
holds them, as the year holds winter
and sweet air of the summer hill.

4. Sioned

Before I took her to wife
I judged the land by yield, its contours
as workable or not, and all it grew
food, shelter or nuisance.

Then she came, smiling, over my threshold.
Sioned, Sioned, said the wind,
that I had never listened to before
except for warning of storm.
From the tyddyn's grudging windows,
creaking door, now when I looked I saw.

Red-brown leaves, that had been nothing
but hint of winter, were warm with her hair's colour;
and in spring the useless bluebells,
that fed no stock, and sent my sled askew,
were for joy now, being her eyes
beneath my gaze.

He had two years, our son, until
his playtime ended, and he lay
fevered and wasting, drooling out
the sips of cawl or milk his mother held
to his white lips. Those weeks
before he died seemed longer
than all his tiny life till then.

She has a way now, on the warmest day
or by the hot winter hearth, of chafing
hand on hand, as though wringing them,
or as if some chill can never let her go.
Stiffly, in duty, she moves from task to task,
lies in our bed.
Sioned, Sioned, cries the wind over the hill,
where close among grasses bluebell leaves
wait for the spring.

5. Landscape with Figures

Behind the house loomed crags of a ravine.
A breeze, shifting, carried watery echoes.
Everything was pervaded by the valley's
extreme, uncompromising beauty. I thought
that there, whatever in the weave
might be harsh, twisted, disproportionate,
must stretch and blend into a balanced pattern.

One man I met there then is dead.
Invaded by a dark he could not speak of,
he cut his life away. The farmer stayed.
Skilled with the whittling-knife, in solitude
he wakes from wood the beasts asleep in it.
Weather and men he meets with taciturn
competence, keeping his counsel, never
risking unguarded boundaries.

Sometimes I see them waving me goodbye,
standing on the yard, their valley lit
superbly by fitful sun; and now see too
how down the ravine white mist would roll
like mercy to cover the suffering house,
and the land's beauty, that was not enough.

6. January Road

Fog and frost are forecast. Cold
has already deepened. Bare hill,
forested hill, rear into mist.
Up the farm road go Landrover,
grey digger with red arm bent back,
blue pick-up. Murky air deceives,
imposing strange perspectives;
from across the stream, climbing vehicles
are magnified to closeness, have startling
immediacy, their colour changing
this weather of despair.

The Landrover is gone
into encroaching white; foot by foot
digger vanishes, like a python's prey;
noisily, little pick-up follows.
Over the mountain the last curl of road
to a ruined house and its living pastures
will be made before cold clenches
too rigidly for prising.

                    Ragged-fringed,
mist drifts lower. From far within it comes,
faintly now, purposeful hum of motors,
long crunch of wheels, clunk of shifted stone,
undaunted music of the bright machines,
already journeying into spring.

7. Silage

Ensiled, the summer grass
rots in black plastic to nourishment
for winter stock. They too
may find that a diminishment,
preferring thrust and juice of growing leaf
on muzzle and tongue, or munchiness
of a rich summer's aftermath
to tease and prickle the mouth.
But hunger does not quibble. Soon,
in white fields or draughty stalls, slavering
they will mumble this rankness, relishing
the soggy harvest of a froward season,
summer less than it might have been,
yet yielding from wind-beaten rainy green,
to fire and flavour winter months,
savour and ferment of hot life.

8. Rights of Way

He guardedly agrees
that the day is fine.
He wonders where I come from,
but will not ask. He thinks
I have left gates open,
and will check. Finding them shut
will not modify his mistrust.

Few make their way up here
to cross his yard between
old house and older barns; one
is too many. He feels as pain
this violation of land, his land,
by ancient custom and prescriptive right.

Diffidently, in cherishing sun,
I cross to the far gate.
Crouched by an ailing tractor,
sidelong he watches.
We are straitly buckled
into antagonistic rôles,
but I wave. Slowly
he raises a hand; turns away.

9. Aspects of Stone

Sandstone country —
not many miles from home, yet the land
has its own vocabulary,
half-alien; not another language,
but an unfamiliar dialect.
The farmhouse down the track
could sit as happily
in a cranny of our moors,
but looks across a steeper valley
to sharper slopes, that hint
at the cliffs not far upstream.

In our valleys, hedges are coaxed
into as rich a growth
as shrivelling wind allows. Here,
field is parted from field
by stone, not wood and leaf,
a pattern of walls diversifying
the texture of grass.

Pure hill-bred
or plumped by a lowland gene,
sheep, driven by impulses of the blood
we construe as cunning or stubbornness,
adapt to their terrain.

The men who work them
are guarded at first meeting
on another's ground;
they live by the idiosyncrasies
of their own patch. Yet they
are of one cousinry, different
from all outside that wary,
humorous, enduring kindred,
but from each other, varying only
as shale from sandy rock,
aspects of stone.

10. The Hedge

Down the side of that sloping field
were old hawthorn trees, tall, wild,
all that was left of a hedge, no use any more
to divide or shelter, with those gaps
between trees, those branchy arches, waist-high,
shoulder-high, framing field or stream.

Now, back-end of the year, farmer and boy
have cut the hawthorn, chain-saw groaning for hours,
great swathes of brushwood fringing a corridor
in which a few branches, spared, are being bent
into a new pleached hedge; stakes driven in,
wire strained, to make a flanking fence.

It will be a good hedge, woven to trim
density, bare slim boughs budding
here and there, pale yellow-green, next spring;
the year after, trying a tentative
blossom again. Before too long
there should be shade and windbreak.

One day, far on, someone may stand
where I am now, across the river,
and say 'That's the old hedge, all run to ruin —
but look at the way those branches frame
parcels and plocks of beauty! Look now —
next winter is the cutting-time'.

(In old deeds, small units of land are sometimes
called 'parcels' or 'plocks'.)

11. What Then?

And if one cottage
grew the best carrots
or one holding
had the best oats
or one hut
was hag-haunted,
what then?

Even their stones
are scattered,
even their bounds
arguable, their people
nameless.

The young
listen to different stories.
What will they tell
when the nights draw in?

There is the life
and telling of the life.
There is completing
and forgetting,
and the offering
of forgotten things.

Waterspout, 1853

They still ask me about the night
when the waterspout burst on Epynt.
I tell them little. It is enough
to have endured such workings of the mind,
to endure them still.

July heat grew heavier as afternoon
deepened; down over Builth the sky
was uneasy with cloud.
Midges thronged itchily by Duhonw stream.
The dog could not settle; prick-eared,
pelt a-twitch, whining,
he stared up at the hills.

Sultry night came. I woke to crazy howling,
clap after vicious clap of storm,
and growling, churning, pouring
greater far than rain.
I splashed across the kitchen,
fought whirlwind to get outside.
Lightning could not stop; it lit
luxuriance of destruction.

Across the demented stream — a torrent now,
tossing trees, rolling rocks, down, down
towards bloated Wye — I saw the house Dôlfach
split open, two contorted trees
passing through it and on.

All I saw, heard, darkly penetrated
all I was. Even now, long after,
I back away from questions. How
could I have helped them, the five who died?
I did not see them, and could not have heard.
Yet whatever years are left me
will be too few to build flood-walls
for my once inundated mind.

'Tall Ships', Gary Hill Video Exhibition

It is as if, at the inner limit of deep water,
a tall ship were to hang, spume-blurred, swollen-sailed,
rippling like a mirage, a looming presence
unforgettably encountered. Veering,
caught by a new wind, she billows away
towards the horizon's possibilities. Bit by bit
she shrinks to a sparkling point far out to sea,
dipping below sight now, freeing the eye
from following, never quite freeing the mind.

The gallery seems entirely black.
'Stand still', says the young custodian,
'wait for the light to grow'. Slowly
down the dark narrow length, separately,
people start to walk out of the wall.
Black-and-white images, men, women,
diverse in race and age, and a girl-child
stretching her arms to plead or welcome,
one by one grow, pause, recede. Like dreams, they question

Far off, there is a man sitting on the ground.
He sees me watching him; unfurls,
moves heavily, deliberately nearer.
Always a little blurred, he looms, confronts me.
Which of us is the moving image?
When I go on, he turns at his leisure,
swings dwindling into distance. He, it seems,
chose when to veer away. My mind
is unfree still, compelled to go riding
the climbing, sliding dream-tides of deep water.

Fantasy

Into dark deepening through two long miles
down to the sea-bed, the observation bubble
would throw a pinched brilliance.
Shapes that swam up, and back to obscurity,
might not be reassuring. Down, down,
beneath huge pressures, in seeming stillness
that is the slow gigantic swing
of the true deep, there I'd find
the black smoker, the towering cloud,
the hell-hot vent of poison
from depths erupting below depths.
On my vulnerable light-path
would appear fish, or things like fish;
crabs, or things like crabs, that only here,
battening only on this volcanic venom,
sidle, flick, suck, gorge.

'What was it like?' I'd be asked,
and not want to answer, since it was like
nothing they could know, except perhaps
the mind; and not many want to sink
deliberately into that dark, to know
those scalding poisons, grotesque encounters.
A poor witness, I'd soon be let alone
to come to terms with what I'd invoked —
like some dusty necromancer who had sought
unchancy knowledge, and now found sleep
not to be wished for; or some Pandora
whose rickety box-lid couldn't be forced back down.

(A black smoker is a volcanic vent in the sea-bed, emitting black
clouds of water at 150 degrees C, full of poisonous chemicals.)

Shapes in Ice

Ice-patterns on the window
have a formal, deliberate beauty,
like illustrations for an Argument from Design.
Now a blade of heat from the fan
begins to carve holes — a round one
through which I can see snow lying,
and now again snow falling;
and a wedge-shaped one, reminding me
of something seen on a journey, thirty years ago.

Windscreen wipers laboured. The beleaguered car
slowly jolted through an Easter blizzard
along the lakeside track; turned steeply uphill,
almost blind in whiteout, to the house Nantybeddau
on its hilltop. Outside, by the door,
lay the stone we had heard of, an arm's length
of dark snow-crusted density, wedge-shaped,
on its wider end blunt incisions
of a problematic alphabet.

I find my photographs, lay two side by side.
One is of the Nantybeddau brothers,
three old men hunched into raincoats,
sheltering in an open shed. Two
are almost smiling; the third
gazes off-right in meditative calm,
one hand abstractedly comforting
his sheepdog's nose. Huge snowflakes
fleck the foreground. Even then
these brothers lived, in their solitude,
a present that was most men's past.
Now they have moved into memory, that in its turn
fades into ultimate snows.

                    The other picture
shows the stone. Vulnerable too — to burial,

drowning, defacing, splitting, doomed
to deconstruction at the End of Things,
it has so far survived, speaking
whatever words each generation gives it.
Unliving, it belongs with the life
of men who cut that ancient message,
those who set it on the river shore
(under lake-water now), and those
who brought it up here, kept it
with a kind of pride.

The shapes blur off the warming window;
puddles trickle to the sill. I see
but will soon forget that Easter snow,
the dark stone at the foot of the wall,
the old men's living eyes, and the cold gentle hand
stroking and stroking the dog's uplifted nose.

No Use

Even if I took him down
to the *aber*, the tumbling
of Gwesyn into Irfon,
so that he could feel
the endlessness of it;

even if I brought to mind
the young stream far in the hills,
the growing river with its meadows,
so that he could feel
the wholeness of it,

he would still be thinking
of pictures in my album — his far-away daughter,
nine years old, in her red jersey,
laughing with her friend
on rocks by the stream.

And even if I took him
into the upper valley,
so that he could feel
the river he'd seen end
constantly beginning,

he'd be no nearer to her.
Failing to catch a flicker of red
over the rocks, he'd suffer
an angry grief. Try as he might,
he wouldn't hear the silent voices laughing.

Emblems

1. Chwefru

He liked that valley.
Old friends, we often made there
small discoveries, like the crab-apples
he would harvest at summer's end.
Too well acquainted with the mind's dark,
he might have had a sombre emblem,
not one like this I fashion from wings and light.

One hot day, high upstream,
we saw, incredulous, on a small stone
in the river, a crowded confabulation
of butterflies, heads together, folded wings
raying out, uncountable angels
on the point of a pin. Beyond, moorland
spread away into the eye of the sun.

There they went, rising in a whirligig,
fluttering into the invisibility
of huge light. I remember how his eyes
tracked them, till tears of dazzle blurred
stream and moor, and the butterflies were gone.

2. Morfa

I remember the marsh flowers,
sharp yellow, soft pink, in the wiry grass.
Crouching to pick them, we children
were lower than the reed-clumps,
could have toppled into clouds
that scudded through sky of pools.
Back of the town, hills reared,
but the Works ruled the flatlands,
beautiful grim shapes dark grey
on yellowed sky by day, and staging at night
the *son et lumière* of emerging steel.

The marsh air was unclear, a confusion
of sweet and salt, earth-exhalation and mist,
at the edge of a familiar miasma
hanging over the town. One day
we saw swans in shining progress
down a reedy channel, sailing locked
to their reflections, that wavered
with a polluted breeze.
                    Summing purity, clarity,
all that was not, the immaculate creatures
joined with our love of the place as it was.
Memory sees what the children did not,
ambivalence and taint; but keeps
all we then had, within one white image.

Olchon Valley

June has lit such a summer fire,
such a fire in the hedges! Sober hazel-leaves,
tipped orange-pink, flare out of green,
burn translucent against the sun.

Once there was lit such a towering fire,
such a fire in the valley! Those who sat,
sober hearers, by hidden hearths, flared
out of homespun and leather, out of curbed flesh,
to spirit, to power, climbing, spreading-
flame the Word lit, words fanned.

Not a flame from that conflagration
breaks out here today, not a drift of its ashes
blurs the black slopes over the valley. But a fire
that was always here at the heart of quiet
gathers us into its congregation.

(The Olchon Valley under the Black Mountains was in the
seventeenth century the refuge of an early Nonconformist
congregation, which had a number of offshoots.)

Not the Pathetic Fallacy

Is it an inescapable vanity
to read speech in the valley's geometry,
see it written in Bryn Mawr's long line
clearly yet untranslatably,
like every word of the sun's decline?

No victim of pathetic fallacy,
you know what these things say
has no connection with what you feel,
can't do the weeping or praising for you,
is not concerned to preach or heal.

It's the next step that's hard to take,
try as you may to break
the illogical link, look and listen anew,
free from this notion of talk
going on all around (though not for you).

July is difficult, Gorffennaf,
month of completion, when you have
just outside the window a poetry
so exuberant, profuse metaphors of leaf
tumbling each over each, desperate imagery.

Content for long now with living
in shade, fertile uncertainty, accepting
mystery, why not give up the fight —
assent to that endless speech, let it cling
to the edge of perception, fading
to distant static, echo of light?

Party Night

There was a party last night at the commune
the other side of the hill. Darkness
was cool, with no wisp of wind
to bring sound this way. Opening the window
I heard only the stream, though a pulse,
hardly perceptible, beat with mine.
To the east, reflected light, too early for dawn,
changed the sky over that other valley.

TV had been in a two-hour time-warp —
twenty-five years back, the Isle of Wight,
'last of the great Festivals'. Hendrix, Baez, the Doors,
drawing the biggest crowd ever, and the tetchiest.
Hope, chicanery, muddle, disillusion —
it all ended in tears. The camera showed some
on Joni Mitchell's face, the microphone
picked up the shake in her voice as she pleaded
with explosive hordes for 'a little respect',
a chance for her music. Last image
was acre on acre of littered wasteland
to sound-track of 'Desolation Row'.

As the night aged, beams of light
burst out intermittently from the high forest,
zigzagged downwards; early leavers
on their way home. Still no sound;
but towards dawn I thought I heard
people talking, a long way off; and the river
weeping away their words.

Back

Out of the forest
with its half-smothered ruins,
we went down to the dried lake
on a track six years under water
since last we found it,
rougher now than then, rougher then
than in the drought before.
We had gentler walking
over the patterned mud,
great orange-red swathes of bistort,
green lane on the further shore.

'We'll come back next time,
won't we?' asked the child.
Next time — one year? ten years?
I said 'If we can'.
That night, black cindered stars
confused me with bright presentness
of their past light, till cloud came over
and the rains began.

Strangeness

There is no excellent beauty that hath not some
strangeness in the proportion. — Francis Bacon

Certainly this is an excellent beauty,
not without strangeness. After the stumbling
down rarely-trodden rides, the last yards
forced through prickly spruce, these dark walls
suddenly rearing in the close dim glade
startle and delight. This is no longer
a house, though it keeps some of that shape.
Fern, fronding lintel, frilling wall,
has joined with stone in symbiosis.
This is a thing both made and grown.
If it outlasts the forest, it will lose
that weird fertility, shadowy dignity.
But for a while yet it yearns upward
from its hidden ground, a votive candle of dark.

Dog on the Hill

I had a dog who feared this hill.
Just where a house once stood,
by a twist of the path up to the ridge,
he would bristle, dip tail and run
all the way back down,
to be splash in the stream,
black blob by home's white walls.
I would go on up the track,
with nothing more to disturb me
than lack of breath.

           This morning at dawn
a trick of mist and light showed the open slope
with a pelt's ripple and sheen; black shelter-belt
wearing a glory; mound and rock throwing
strangest of shadows, like walls;
all about to change, all never to change.

Poor dog, poor beast with few graces,
perhaps he knew, the whole time,
whatever briefly touched my eyes
with unsustainable clear-sight;
whatever now at thinning of mist,
flattening of light, has gone back.

Naked

There are monasteries on crags.
One, left empty
by the last of its monks,
still had a fragile bridge
pilgrims cautiously crossed,
till it weakened, crashed
into the chasm.
On the pinnacle, out of reach,
chapel walls make unseen
their offering of flaking frescoes,
broken cells hold unheard
echoes from years of prayer.

Perhaps the monks wept
for their lost home, knowing
how long a dying was its doom,
yet knowing the irrelevance
of that stripping-away;
as when at the source of the Ganges
two priests celebrated Mass —
the wind blew out the candles,
the river drowned the words.
There were no clothes now
for the naked prayer,
that leapt up the rocks
and triumphing climbed the gale.

Words to Say

i.m. L.B.

I turn the diary pages to this month,
November, one hundred and forty years ago.
To the north-east, over those hills, a moor,
a house on the slope beyond; a man
plodding over a darkening desolation.
This was the first time I ever crossed
the boggy high tableland
of Rhôs Saith Maen. So it still is —
the Seven Stones deeper into peat, the miles
long and soggy, evening lights ahead
still welcome.

    A house full of children;
one girl beautiful. Next autumn he wrote
Her breathing is short; her face much flushed;
she has a most unnatural cough.
He had no need to explain his fear. By spring,
hope was thin and fading. October brought snow,
the most raging storm for years. He dreaded
November, sinking of the light.
Marianne now never quits her bed. Soon
the black grandeur of thirty mounted mourners
brought meagre consolation, being appropriate,
like the eulogy he thought fitting for this page,
private, yet ready for a future eye:
The charms of beauty, amiableness and virtue
had here met. She could not be beheld
without admiration and love.

There are other sicknesses now, and less
expansive words. November closes in. Still
of the untimely dead there is need to say
that she was happy and loved, and has gone away.

Into the Dark

The last Roman soldier is thought to have left Wales by 400 A.D.
The six people in this poem speak from points in the uneasy years
spanning that departure.

1. Fort

I had a fancy only yesterday
that they were marching out
for the last time — perky,
but a bit ragged. Once there were fewer
of these wild lads from who knows where —
more of the real Romans. Gods!
how they would swing down the good roads!
I grant you this Roman Peace
pinches us sharply; and mercy
is a word most of them don't know —
remember poor Cradoc,
who sold the Commandant light weight?

But it *is* peace, if you take their way of it.
And who would want the tribes'
knives in the night? Some here
have daughters, too, who would cry
to see the Legion go.
The fort is busy enough; the trumpet
brisks and firms the hours. So why
do I keep dreaming of departure?

2. Leaving the Villa

I have never been back. At first
I hungered for the place. Sybilla,
our daughter, was born there;
all of us loved it,
the small villa under a hill
in the misty western land.

I knew we'd have to leave,
before Marcus told me,
one evening while Sybilla slept.
The farm was dying. Market roads
had roughened to pot-holed tracks,
and our men hung back, hearing
too many tales of plunder. Death
could pounce from any thicket,
lurk round any bend.

We're safe now, surely,
in the noise and cramp of Moridunum?
Marcus in mercy killed my dreams of home,
telling me of the changes — a corn-kiln
intruding in our long calm room, that looked
over green distance beyond the colonnade:
our bedchamber a store: the dolphin mosaic
(rustic, but always my pride) now broken.

Soon, I think, I shall forget.
Only it seems that unreality
threatens all places now, like mist
waiting its chance to swallow up the hill,
like death waiting on every road.

3. Change

Master from here, master from off,
what difference?
Rain is master,
quick shudder of bog,
rot of hoof, rot of udder.
Sun is master,
waterless craving,
swelling of tongue,
gadfly madness.
What change can be?

Change is rain after sun,
spring after winter,
young man's hand
now ruling old man's horse.
Change leads round and back
and is unchanging.
What other?

I watch my sheep
on the dark hill.
When eyes weary
or a young dog fails,
some wander.
Stumbling and broken,
or throat ripped
by the red slinker, they end
in stench, swarming, white scatter.
What change can be?

From under my ewes'
dungy draggle-tails
I squeeze the heavy milk.
The woman whirls and lumps it
to butter and soft fat cheese.
The woman hears talk of change
building like thunder.

Master from here, master from off,
what difference?
All are mastered
by hill's weather,
by body's forcing,
years' withering.
But the woman is restless.
When she asks
'What change is coming?'
I have no answer.

4. Mithraeum

Sunk into the hilltop
was the soldiers' shrine,
the temple of Mithras,
doubly forbidden to me,
a girl and native to this place.

The whole of that small hill was banned.
I would see on the ridge a light
spread faintly up, among the trees,
when some door below ground
opened for a moment.
They would climb the hill
in silent groups. Sometimes I saw
the Bull going up to die; it was said
they drank his blood.

Suddenly, they were all gone —
the fort empty, dung left to dry
in the stables, granary doors
creaking in an edgy wind.
Fear was there, shapeless and dense.
In the dark Mithraeum, open to me now,
fear again, and cold, and a huge absence.
I wished I knew an invocation
even to him, no god of mine: a prayer
for times of terror. But I was dumb
before his ashy altars,
and ran up into the sun.

5. Victim

We poured down her small throat
a drench of sleep-herb.
She gagged, but swallowed,
and still she screamed.
At last the sound
shrank to a scraping whisper,
then only her jagged breath.

After, we bound the stump
with blood-herb, fever-herb.
Three days, three nights
she was gone from us
into a darkness where
her mother bled and died
a hundred times, and flames
for ever licked and crunched
her childhood.

Can I say
she is healed now? The dreams
come less often, and she is skilled
at her hop-and-grab journeys
from stool to pallet, or to crouch
by the patched hearth.

Surely these are the world's
last years. Our children
tear us with pity and guilt,
being sad inheritors of so little life
and so much hurt.

6. Supplication

On the altar-stone
bread of pain,
bitter cup.

I lift my hands
to the Threefold,
call down
the change, the joy.
The small cold mass-house
trembles with power.

Into this dark
I pray we go down
as into a holy well,
as into black waters
of healing.

In this ending
I pray we know
newness.

After this rending
I pray we find
wholeness.

Through this fire
I pray we leap
into peace.

Acknowledgements

We would like to thank the Editors of the following publications where these poems first appeared: *Planet, Poetry Wales, The Malahat Review, The New Welsh Review, Window on Wales*. 'Catherine at Stouthall' and 'Beaupré Castle' both appeared initially in the anthology, *The Third Day: The Landscape and the Word*, ed. by Kathy Miles, (Gomer, 1995). 'Bluetit Feeding' also appears in the Seren Anthology, *Burning the Bracken: Fifteen Years of Seren Poetry*, (1996).